67

by

Larry A. Yff

Table of Contents

Introduction

I can honestly say every book I've written so far came from out-of-the-blue; meaning it wasn't planned. They all came from the Holy Spirit tapping my shoulder and saying, "You should open up and be honest about your porn addiction. Maybe help someone by putting it in a book?" or "Hey, remember that interesting story you read about in the Bible that helped you? Maybe help someone by putting it in a book?" or "You did some crazy shit and God brought you out of it. Maybe help someone by putting it in a book?" and then it would all come together and a book would be written.

Not this one. This one wasn't forced...but it was. I realized I had 66 books in my Bible-based series. What? You don't see my dilemma, Reader? 66 books. The Bible is a 66-book series. By me writing a 66-book, Bible-based series, I didn't want it to seem

planned.

I would hate for people to say, "Look at him. That mutha

fucka thinks He's better than God or somethin'! He wrote his own

66-book, God-inspired series! Who in the fuck does he think he

is? You know he used to smoke crack and look at some seriously

nasty porn shit, don't you?"

Well, to avoid that, I've decided to write "67". This is the

67th book and it will be about all the crazy, bad, nasty, good, weird

shit that comes across my mind every day. Some of it is shit I

really did and other stuff is what I've fantasized and other stuff is

what I've witnessed. What it all has in common is it helped me

understand or get through different phases in life.

We've all been through some crazy, but I think we need to

start sharing more things, not necessarily all the crazy, so we can

help others get through situations. That's what I love about the

Bible: there are enough crazy stories about sex, alcohol, incest,

murder, riches, marriage and war that I can see things to avoid

and how to avoid them or I can see how they got through

problems I'm facing. Ready? Check it out. Book 67...

Big Dick Problems

So, I have a nice-sized dick. I do, but a guy my wife was dating some time before me had a bigger dick and I couldn't get that shit out of my head for a long time. It even affected our sex life at 1st.

Oh, how did I know he had a bigger dick than me? She told me. Can you believe that, Reader? She told me, but I have to admit, it was me that got that dumb ass conversation started.

Her and I started off our relationship being as honest as possible and bearing our souls. On my end, I had no choice: she saw me smoking crack and staring at porn. If I wanted her to remain in my life or be a part of it, I had some early explaining to do, so I did.

It's been good and bad, but mostly good. It's been mostly good because reality is reality and we've all done and had things prior to getting into our current relationship, so we have to be able to "accept the things we cannot change, have the courage to change the things we can and the wisdom to know the difference." His dick was bigger than mine and I had the wisdom to understand there was nothing I could do to change that so I had to accept it.

It's not like I thought about his dick a lot...just every time I looked at her and got horny! I would look at her and want to jump her bones and then...then I would remember she liked it when he jumped her bones and then I would lose that hot spark until that image and thought was out of my head.

I look at her a lot, like several times a day, so I guess I actually did think about his dick more than I think, now that I'm thinking about it.

I want to be her all. Her 1st husband. Her best friend. Her dream-man. Her everything and, well, that includes wanting to be her best lover.

Men and women think in different terms sexually and it's natural. I can't imagine what it would be like to have some guy bending me over or me riding him or getting pregnant and having some "thing" growing inside of me until it comes out and tears my uterus open; however, *I can* imagine bending some hot chick over or *her* riding me or *her* getting pregnant and having some "thing" growing inside of *her* until it comes out and tears *her* uterus open.

Men are visual when it comes to sex because our "sex part" is visual. I'm basically trying to give a rationale explanation for why men think with their dicks.

Since we think with our dicks, some of us get dick size mixed up with love. A lot of us men grew up with porn on our phones or like I did back in the day, looking at nudey-magazines.

Either way, the concept we were being taught was love, or at least sex, was based on dick size.

In porn, the guy always has a big dick or he appears to have a big dick. Females always talk about the camera adds 10 pounds to your appearance and maybe the camera adds a couple of inches to dick size?

That part I don't know, but what I did learn from porn and Playboy magazines was:

1. All the men had big dicks

2. In order to be in porn you had to have a big dick

3. The women all wanted the big dick

4. The women loved to have a dick so big it could barely fit in their mouth, pussy or asshole

And that's where I got the concept of the essentials and necessity for a big dick. Without one, you were just wasting her time and yours. A big dick was apparently what was needed to really satisfy a woman.

A big dick was apparently what they wanted.

A big dick paid the bills.

A big dick can make a female ignore your looks, the fact that you still live with your mama or that you don't have a job.

A big dick makes everything better. It's like that Frank's Hot Sauce commercial where they say, "I put that shit on everything!"

I have a nice-sized dick. It's definitely not the biggest and it's definitely not the smallest, so I'm definitely happy with it. Well, I was until she told me about one of her big-dick ex-boyfriends!

I wanted to be her big-dick lover.

I wanted to give her some good porno dick that I thought all women wanted.

I wanted to give her the dick that basically impaled her and made her scream in pleasure and pain.

I wanted that because I was leaving the fantasy life of porn and strip-clubs and I thought that's what I was supposed to do and since I couldn't do that, I thought I was a failure. I figured she would pretend to be happy sexually because we're married, but she would probably be secretly ordering "dick grow" pills, grinding them up and putting them in my food.

I just realized I told you I didn't think about his big dick a lot and here I am already on page 8 talking about it and I probably have another 8 more pages to go! I don't mind. It's life and I'm probably not the only one who had to deal with it…

So, I'm deep in my porn addiction at the beginning of our marriage still and I'm trying to get out of the porn fantasy sex and into having sex with a real female. It was touch and go because I

would be turned on, but every time she would touch my dick it

would go limp. I know! I know! Trust me! I know!

She shoulda left me and probably woulda left me if it

wasn't for God. We both love God and made sure we got married

in a real church by a real pastor, not in a roadside chapel by

someone dressed like Elvis Presley. She and I both knew we were

in this and accountable to God. No easy exits.

For me it started with understanding the realities of sex

better and I asked her why she left this particular ex and what did

she like about him. She laid it out pretty simply: she liked his big

dick and she left him because of his big dick. What the fuck?

Explain, please!

"Well, he wasn't the best-looking guy," she started off,

"but we were cool...and he had a big dick."

"Okay," I said, "so what was the problem again?"

"Well, he figured that was all he needed to keep me and I had to prove him wrong. Can't no dick keep me! It was that plus some other shit…but mostly that."

So now, looking to "accept the things I cannot change" I asked her how is it you women can hate a guy but stay with him because he has a big dick? Is it that serious and would you consider leaving me since I don't have the big dick?

She said it's not that serious…but it is. Explain, please!

The bottom line was, according to her, you had to be able to please her sexually, but you had to have more than that. You had to have some God in your life and some motivation to live life on God's terms somehow.

Lucky for me, he wasn't in the spiritual place he needed to be or she would have been off with him, getting her vagina blew out and probably had about 4 more kids by now! Ain't God good, y'all?!? Yes He is! All the time, God is so good!

You may be wondering why I was torturing myself and wanting to know the ins and outs of her exes and all those private details that I shouldn't give a fuck about, right? Like I told you, I was coming off a 20-year run of having sex with strippers and watching pornos. Encountering a real pussy scared the shit out of me and my dick and now that I was married…I couldn't afford to try and give my wife "the scared dick".

Everybody processes things differently and that's why I'm sharing with you so you can see as many different angles and views on a subject so you can see something that may help you. I don't suggest you male Readers start diggin' too deep and asking your wives how many dicks has she had, who was her best lover and did any of them have a bigger dick than you. That may not be for you…

In fact, my process may be a one-of-a-kind process and if so, that's cool. If you can't learn from my process, that's cool too. What I want you to be able to take away from my process is certain realities. There are certain realities about sex, porn and marriage that need to be shared and discussed openly.

Should I be ashamed that his dick is bigger than mine? No, because the reality is there will always be a bigger dick out there than yours.

Should I be ashamed that I felt insecure and that I wouldn't be able to satisfy my wife? No, because the reality is a lot of people in marriages have sexual issues and concerns that should be talked about but no one does. Next thing you know, some female is calling in about her husband beating her ass and nobody knows why.

I know why! She's not happy sexually and you both know it, but nobody's talking. To top it off, she's got a guy at work she's fucking and you both know it but nobody's talking. Taking it one step further, that last baby may not be the husband's baby and you both know it, but nobody's talking.

Next thing you know, he snaps and beats his wife ass and now all the details come out about how he doesn't know who his biological dad is because his mama was cheating. You just never know, so put your pride aside and share some shit to help as many people as you can. Worst case scenario, it will help you to get some stuff out your system that's been causing you to doubt yourself, your relationship and your sanity.

I went on a rambling spree, but I'm pretty sure before I went off into left field we were talking about, ummmm, "the scared dick". We were talking about the scared dick and how I had to get comfortable with the reality of a real-life, wet vagina that could possibly give me an STD, a baby or both. You can't catch an STD from porn. You can from a stripper though...

At a strip-club, the stripper girl you're about to have sex with sees your dick and doesn't care anything about it because your dick doesn't matter: she wants to make money off you paying her for sex or just lusting after her.

In a porn, the video girl never sees your dick and doesn't care anything about it because your dick doesn't matter: she wants to make money off you buying her video.

My wife sees my dick she loves sex and my dick matters: she wants to have real sex and make real babies. This isn't just some lustful fuckin' or casual "see you later" sex. Sex is something that can be a deal-breaker for a casual relationship, but for a marriage where you have kids, houses and bank accounts together…it could be a 50-year death sentence.

This marriage thing was new. It was real. It was my 1st introduction into a committed, long-term relationship that was gonna involve a whole lot of sex and I was nervous. I wanted to spend as much time in the Research and Development stage as possible.

With porno sex and strip-club sex there are no arguments, discussions, crying babies, emotional wives, bills that need to be paid, jealous boyfriends calling or driving by the house. It's just sex. It's just sex with no rules, boundaries, laws or guidelines and to be honest…that shit sucks!

Once I got used to life with a real vagina and all the ups and downs of dealing with its female owner, I loved it! I loved it and there's no way I'm going back to pornos and strip-clubs for some bullshit fantasy sex.

So, I guess if I was going to share this story and provide you with some lessons, I would summarize them up as being:

1. Porn is the worst teacher for sex education

2. Don't fall in love with a stripper

3. The best sex is marriage sex

4. You can only give her what you got

5. If you got a big dick, swipe that thing like it's a credit card every chance you get! From what I hear, it's as good as cash

Family Sex

Since sex is such an important topic and has fucked up a lot of homes, relationships and marriages, I thought I would touch on it one more time, from a different angle, and then get into some other random-ass topic...

The tv preacher named Joyce Meyer said her dad had sex with her every weekend from the time she was a "young girl" until she was 18. Can you believe that shit!? Can you believe she is a pastor and has no problem admitting that craziness in front of millions of viewers?

I love it! I love her boldness! I love her bravery! I love the fact that FINALLY somebody in the church publicly admitted to going through some crazy shit growing up. It was not only crazy shit...it was sex shit!

If I could have whispered that last part about "it was sex shit!" I would have. I would have because people in the church don't talk about sex. I haven't seen any preachers in real life or on the television that look like they're having fun sex.

I take that back: they're not having boring sex! I don't see no passion or romance…nothing! The 1st ladies have shirts that go up to their chins and the bottoms cover their ankles and there is nothing sexxxy or romantic about that shit!

I'm not saying I want my wife to show her titties with a crop-top and let them boys see her nice ass by wearing tight jeans…but at the same time, shit, relax and show whatchoo got! Woman thou art loosed! Thou art loosed from the boring, un-sexy, Amish-lookin' outfits you've got on!

Joel Osteen has a hot wife. TD Jakes daughter, Sarah Roberts is attractive as well, so the rest of you non-fuckin' pastor-couples better thank those 2 women every time you see them.

They bring beauty, classy sexxxy and God's Word to the pulpit. Take some notes.

I know a pastor who appears to have everything going for him. He's a pastor and his dad was a pastor. His parents were happily married for 50 years or so. He's married to his wife and they have been happily married for maybe 40 years or so…and he was almost charged with rape.

Yup, he was almost charged with rape because he was over 18 and she was younger than 18. She had a kid and everything. They did a blood test and found out it wasn't his, so he didn't catch a case.

Here's my thing: nobody in the church knows and if they do know, nobody's sharing these types of experiences. Everybody's walking around like their pastor never made some choices that maybe weren't the best. Everybody's walking around like he's an angel. Everybody's walking around like he's a saint and that's what we tend to do with pastors until...until they fall the fuck off!

One pastor revealed he had a phone-sex addiction and was spending $1000 a month. To avoid being confronted in front of his congregation he killed himself.

The gospel singer Kirk Franklin admitted, after his wife busted him, that he had a secret porn stash that had at least 1,000 DVD pornos! Sticking with him as an example, he was recorded in a conversation with his son and formally apologized.

In the conversation, his son and him had an argument and then Kirk told his son that, "...you better shut the fuck up before I break your mutha-fuckin' neck, bitch! Do you know who the fuck you're talkin' too?"

He apologized and I was disappointed. Why apologize? You're human? You get mad like anybody else. You cuss like anybody else? You lose your temper like everyone else. Speaking of a pastor and his temper…

The well-known pastor named Creflo Dollar had to go to court for apparently choking his daughter or doing something physical to her. I'm not sure about that whole situation, but everyone was acting all shocked. Why? Something tells me that wasn't his 1st time and something else tells me people in the church been knew he had no problem preaching on Sunday and cussing somebody out on Friday.

So Joyce Meyer was having sex with her dad every weekend for years. She said her mom and a lot of relatives and family members knew it, but nobody said shit! Nobody said shit because 1) it's embarrassing as fuck, 2) it's nasty and dirty as fuck and 3) it's embarrassing, nasty and dirty as fuck! Okay, but it happens…

Nobody wants to admit that kind of shit is happening in their families, but it is and it does. Every day in America and around the world there's some type of nasty, sex-related activity happening and nobody wants to talk about it. Why?

I'm with Joyce: let that shit out! It holds you back. It stunts your mental and spiritual growth. It causes depression and suicide. Get that shit out!

I got fucked in my ass one time when this older boy molested me. I was about 5ish and he was about 18ish. I told my parents and they didn't believe me. They had the boy and his parents come over and we all sat and talked about it, but since I wasn't able to talk about it in grown-up words, nobody believed me. I thought nobody believed me until I was older…

I was talking with one of my big sisters and that topic came up somehow. When I told her about it, she said, "Oh! That makes perfect sense! Around that time, that family just upped

and moved away!"

What that means to me is I wasn't the 1st boy he molested

and to avoid having charges pressed against them and/or their

son, they took the coward way out and left town. They left town

and as far as anybody knew, nothing happened. It was swept

under the rug.

It was swept under the rug until I damn near killed myself

on a weekly basis trying to do as much cocaine as I could because

I hated myself. I hated the fact that I was turned on to looking at

pornos where young girls were getting fucked in the ass. It turned

me on and every time I watched it, I was equally turned on and

sickened.

I finally had to get real and see what the fuck was it that

turned me on and why. I began to realize it had something to do

with being molested one time: I was taken advantage of sexually by an adult and maybe, deep down, I wanted to do that to some young girl. Maybe, deep down, I could relive that incident but this time, I was the one in control. Maybe, deep down, it would help me understand how an adult could do that to a little kid.

Whatever the reason was, I was making it worse and complicated with cocaine. When I was high, I was able to open up about it and at the same time, be sexually turned on to it.

The point is, I only got molested one time and it drove my black ass crazy! Imagine how someone feels who has been 1) raped or molested as an adult and can process and remember things more clearly or 2) raped or molested as an adult on multiple occasions! That mutha fucka needs some serious help and nobody's helping!

The church ain't helping. If they tried to help, it would look hypocritical because priests are in the news every week getting caught and charged for raping and molesting the little boys under their supervision.

Joyce Meyer. She never had help as a young lady and never had closure until her dad died. She made a vow to not share this shit until he was dead. She was living with this trauma for decades!

I recently found out about an older lady who was in a similar and probably worse situation. I say worse because her dad was molesting her since she was around 8 years old and she didn't mind. She said she didn't mind all those years because he was gentle!

What in the fuck!?! You don't think she has mental issues and needs help?! She has been able to rationalize been raped and molested for years because "he was gentle"!?!?

He was gentle, but at the same time, she had multiple abortions! Her sorry-ass, bitch-ass daddy fucked his own little daughter and made her destroy her young body with multiple abortions! If I was her uncle and found out, I would have killed him!

Do you see how angry I am? That's why nobody wants to open up and share that shit. People can get killed really quickly if they are caught molesting little kids...but it happens more than you think. That happens and so does sex-trafficking of little girls and boys.

I know the boy's name who molested me and if I ever came across him in real life, I would want to murder him. I could torture him for weeks and give him a slow death. I could tie any of his sons up and do the same and still sleep good at night.

People need to talk.

People need help with this sex shit.

Somebody needs to stand up and get the party started. So far, Joyce is that one and I give her all the credit and props I can give.

Wanna hear a twist? Even though I could easily torture and murder my molester…I could have easily been one! I came close to being a child molester and that's when I was able to, by getting close to God, get off the 1st exit I saw!

I was getting high and looking at young girls in pornos.

I was getting high and having young girls strip for me and I could have EASILY let it go from stripping to fuckin'.

I was getting high and paying the youngest and the youngest-looking strippers for lap-dances and sex.

I was SOBER and began looking at young girls who I would have easily had sex with if I could have done it and not gotten caught.

The title of this section is "Family Sex". I have shared some personal stuff and stuff I've heard about where family members were having sex and there's more…

I was adopted at birth. Around the time I was 23-years old or so, I went out of State to meet a lot of my biological relatives and family. While I was there, I was attracted to one of them and we had sex. We knew we were related…but didn't care.

We had sex and I was in love! I wanted to marry her! I was making plans to marry her and move to the Bahamas!

Am I a pervert?

Am I a one-of-a-kind guy?

Am I the only person who was ever sexually attracted to a close family member?

Am I the only person who was sexually attracted to a close family member and had sex?

There are so many questions that need to be asked and answered.

There are so many people who need to get help with sex-related issues that aren't able to and it's driving the cost of pussy sky-high. The more secretive, dirty and perverse an activity is, the more it costs.

Child sex-trafficking rakes in billions a year in revenue because billions of people want to have sex with little kids and are willing to pay for it...but they don't want anybody to find out, so they are willing to pay in private.

The porn industry makes billions a year in revenue because billions of people are addicted to fantasy sex and I'm betting most of them have a fucked-up sex life and family life or have no real sex life or family life.

Strippers can make thousands of dollars a night because of lust and sexual addictions. Men are addicted to sex, fantasy sex and/or pornos and they are willing to go to strip-clubs and pay these women so the woman will dance on the guy's lap or let him lick her butt, grab her butt, lick on her titties or grab her titties, give him a hand-job or take him to a booth in the back and have sex with him.

It's nothing new! This shit has been happening forever and that's what I love about the Bible! The various authors in the Bible openly shared stories that weren't the most discreet and they help. These stories help us see 1) how God deals with sex and 2) how we aren't animals and perverts because we can't control our sex and keep our legs closed or our dicks in our pants.

The Bible is one of the most historically accurate history books in the world, so when it talks about some crazy sex shit, you know it has to be true. Check it out...

Crazy Bible Sex

People who hate God and the Bible are quick to say the Bible is a horrible book. I've heard it's horrible because it has more stories about sex and murder than any other book in the world...and they may be right.

They may be right that it has a lot of sex and murder in it, but no more than a typical episode of a much loved and approved television series called "Law and Order" or "CSI: Miami" or any movie starring Samuel Jackson.

In fact, I have to say the "blood and sex" stories are what make the Bible more of an educational book and less of a "holier-than-thou" book. The church needs to be more like the Bible. Here's some stories Bible critics may be referring to:

There was a man named Lot who was the nephew of the famous Abraham. Lot was living in a city that God hated and it was about to be destroyed. The night before it was to be destroyed, 2 angels visited him and apparently they were very good-looking.

We know this because Lot's neighbors all wanted to fuck the 2 angels and I'm talking about man-on-man, homosexual activity. Anyways...

The angels are in the house with Lot and Lot tries to convince the townsmen to leave the 2 new guys alone. Lot tells them they are his guests and that if they wanted to have sex with somebody, rather than disrespect his guests, he would bring his 2 virgin daughters outside and they could all fuck his daughters!

In the end, nobody gets fucked and God destroys the cities of Sodom and Gomorrah for their homosexual behavior and a bunch of other shit. But that's not all regarding Lot and sex.

He had sex with his 2 daughters. Let me tell you the whole story before you judge him...

While God was destroying the town Lot lived in, Lot and his daughters were able to get away. The angels told them to head towards the mountains and not look back.

Once they were settled in, Lot's oldest daughter wasn't happy. She wasn't happy because she wasn't sure how long they were going to be stuck in the cave and that meant no sex and no sex meant no babies. She wanted a baby.

She waited until her dad got drunk one night, she snuck in his tent and they had sex with no condoms. How that happened where he didn't know he was having sex with his daughter, but, whatever…

She gets pregnant and has a baby. The younger daughter got "baby fever" and did the same thing: she waited till her dad got drunk one night, she snuck in his tent and they had sex with no condoms. How that happened where he didn't know he was having sex with his daughter, but, whatever…

She also gets pregnant and has a baby. Maybe the Bible critics are right that the Bible has some crazy sex shit in it, but I applaud the authors for including these stories. These stories link us with people who lived thousands of years before us and still got caught up in sex scandals.

Another sex scandal Bible critics may be talking about is the one where the guy got his head chopped off. I'll tell you the story…

John the Baptist told the King that he, the king, shouldn't be having sex with his own brother's wife. The king didn't like John spreading these rumors, so he had him locked up.

Meanwhile, the king's sister-in-law who he was fucking was not content. She thought it was best that John be killed. She set up an elaborate plan around sex: her lover, the king, would have a birthday party and at the party her daughter would dance

for him, woo him, get him sexually aroused and then the queen
would exact her revenge on John's snitchin' ass

The king has his birthday party and his erotic dance. His
step-daughter is dancing like a stripper and he is absolutely
turned on and horny. When she is done, he tells her she can have
anything up to half of his kingdom! Seriously? One dance and
your dumb-ass is gonna give up half of your dumb-ass kingdom?

When she looks to her mom, her mom motioned for her
daughter to come to her. She approaches her mom, her mom
whispers something in her ear and she jumps back in disgust.
She's disgusted, but she gets her composure and approaches the
king...

"So, sir. You said I can have anything I want, correct? You
actually said I can have up to half of your kingdom, right? Well,
what I want is the head of the man they call John the Baptist. He
is in your prison as we speak."

The king wanted to shut John up, but not cut his fucking head off! A deal is a deal and besides, he told her she could have whatever she wanted in front of everybody. He tells the guards to go to John's cell, they cut his head off and bring the freshly severed, bloody head on a silver platter and hands it to the young lady.

What she did with it, nobody knows. All we know for sure is:

1. She can dance pretty good

2. The king had a thing for young girls…even if it was his stepdaughter

There was another crazy sex story about a man who slept with his daughter-in-law. He was out and about one day and saw a prostitute hanging around and he asked her to come over. She walks over to him and he says he wants to have sex with her but he doesn't have any money on him.

She said he didn't need any money. All he needed was to let her hold his family-crested ring and when he got his money together, he knew where to find her to give her her money and he would then get his ring back. He gives her the ring and he has some prostitute sex.

Later on, he hears that his single, widowed daughter-in-law is pregnant. He calls her disgraceful and wants to have her killed. She thought she was disgusting and disrespectful. "How could you be out here selling your body like a prostitute and get pregnant by some pervert?!?"

She begs for mercy, reaches under her robe and pulls out his family-crested ring. When he asks her how'd she get it, she said, "Do you want to talk about this in private or do you want me to tell all your business right here in the open?" He pulls her aside...

She then explains to him since he lied to her and didn't give any of his other sons to her after her husband, his oldest son died, she decided to take matters into her own hands. She deserved to have a baby that carried the same bloodline as her dead husband's.

She knew he liked prostitutes so she dressed up like one and had sex with him and he gave her the ring as a down payment. He's shocked and embarrassed, but I'll bet he was also impressed with her. She has the baby and that's all we hear about that story.

I think that story ended with some boring, chronological shit that tied that baby in with some other well-known events or with somebody who became famous. I'm not really sure. My point is to highlight the "Crazy Bible Sex", so that's what I did.

We have all heard of King David. Well, he had a son who fell in love. He fell in love with his half-sister. He lusted for her and wanted her so bad, he literally got physically sick. He had to have that!

He has one of his cousins help lure her over to his house under the premise that he's sick and needs her help. She comes over and he rapes her. Once he rapes her, his lust is gone and he can't stand the sight of her and kicks her out his house.

Their other brother finds out and is pissed to the highest degree. He's pissed, but he's also patient. He waits a couple of years and then kills his little brother.

As you can see, the Bible critics do have a point, like I said that there's a lot of nasty, freaky, freaky, nasty stuff in the Bible. Does that mean it's a horrible book? What about all the hot, steamy television series we see that have all the exact same shit in them?

If somebody was to take the entire Bible and give it a different name and make a tv series out of it...damn! I'll bet that will be the top-rated series after the 2nd episode! *Especially* if the producer can accurately say, "All stories are based on actual events".

Bible critics also love to point out all the murders and bloodshed, not just the sex stuff, as casting doubt and negativity on the Bible. There are a lot of murders that are kind of grotesque and ugly, but they are pretty much like anything you will see on most network television shows that are rated PG-13.

So, whatever you want to say about the Bible and try and call it a horrible book because it accurately told stories of real-life people involved in real life situations can kiss my ass. They can kiss my entire, black-ass! I love it!

These stories have helped me relate to people who were not perfect, had God in some aspect of their lives and what that aspect looked like. Doing that allows me to see what the possibilities, rewards and consequences could be for me when I go through similar situations.

I was able to watch God achieve a purpose through the crazy and it helped. I had a lot of crazy sex shit going on in my life and God's still with me and if he can still use a guy who got his two, young daughters pregnant...the odds of Him using me are pretty good and that feels good!

God, Crystal Meth, Death...and more Sex

I know a musical genius. I know him personally and I'm glad I know him personally. If I didn't, I would think of him only as an artistic mix of Prince, Tupac and AC/DC. I know him personally, so I know more than that.

I know he loves God and pussy. I know he wants to impact the entire music industry with his music and his love for God. I know there is an inner conflict going on between his love of God and his love of his talents...and he's not the only one.

"...and then you let me cum on your face..."

"...the smoke, the crystal, the cocaine..."

"...I fuck her good! I fuck her hard! I'm her bad boy!"

He wrote these lyrics and he loves God, Jesus and he has

no problem asking me to pray with him so we both stay focused.

See anything wrong with this picture, Reader?

I see nothing wrong with it and neither does he and that's

where I'm mixed. I'm mixed and so is he. We're mixed because

we don't think your art has to be a certain way if you love God

and him and I are proof.

I added myself to the equation because we both freely

love God and we both freely have no problem cussing and that's a

problem, for Christians only and that's a problem. Him and I have

talked about this several times and the crazy thing is, we're cool

with it and we want the world to be cool with.

Why can't I love God and workout to Tupac music??

Why can't I love God and listen to music that talks about

fucking some girl good and hard??

Why can't I love God and write a book called "Fuck that fig tree!!!"??

Why can't I love God and say "shit" or "fuck"??

Seriously, him and I are both artists and we are both serious about God and will continue to do our craft as God moves us and we don't want Christians to miss out, but we're both sure many will and that's a shame.

This topic here is more about questions then answers because him and I don't have all the answers. He wants to work with a couple of famous artists, but they are the some of the same ones who talk about having a lot of problems but a bitch ain't one and bitches ain't nothin' but hoes and tricks. Is that gonna make God mad?

I'm gonna say no. I'm gonna say no because an artist's work, if it's genuine, will reflect something the artist has gone through or has thought about. The musical artist in this topic has never done Crystal Meth, but he has seen the effects of drug addiction. I don't know if he's ever shot cum on a female's face like his lyrics talk about…but I'm guessing he either has or he's thought about it.

In my book "Fuck that fig tree!!! – a Jesus Story", I write about the fact that I think Jesus used cuss words when He got angry just like anybody else. I don't think He said "oh shoot" instead of "oh shit". I'm saying that because He preferred to run in the alleys and trenches where people who needed help lived at.

Religious leaders were always getting mad at Him for hanging around "scum". It was their belief they were supposed to learn about God and then make the "scum" clean themselves up and then come learn about God at the temples and churches. They felt like they didn't need to "lower" themselves and get on the scum's level and speak how they spoke.

People speak differently…and that's okay.

Some people say "oh shit" and some say "oh shoot" ...and that's okay.

Some people say "orgasm" or "ejaculate" while others say "cum" or "bust a nut" ...and that's okay.

My whole point with this topic is to express my view on creativity in the arts. If you're a writer and you love God, you should be able to express what God is to you in your own words. If you're a musician and you love God, you should be able to express what God is to you in your own words.

I'm just saying it's okay, in my view, to express your life's experiences in your words and in your way whether you are into God or not and nobody should be able to condemn you for that. I love an artist called Lil Wayne.

He makes music about drugs, guns, gang-shit and sex and I love his music. I love his music and I also love God and I don't think there's nothing wrong with that.

I have a question for you Readers out there: do any of you only listen to church music? Have you ever listened to rap or heavy metal music? How did it make you feel?

Personally, I used to feel guilty. I used to feel guilty when I wanted to work out and listen to Tupac instead of Kirk Franklin. I felt guilty because I thought people who love God aren't supposed to talk like Tupac talked or understand things that Tupac understood or bob my head to the beat of music Tupac made.

To feel that way is hypocritical. It's saying Tupac and other artists who write about their lives are scum. It's saying they don't have a relationship with God. It's saying they deserve to be locked up. It's saying their view, experiences, joys and pains in life are irrelevant and don't mean shit and neither do they.

I'm gonna encourage you to keep your relationship with God and:

1. Feel free to say shit or fuck

2. Feel free to listen to Tupac, NWA or Def Leppard when
   you work out at the gym

3. Feel free to compose something about your life and
   share it, even if people may think your view and
   experiences don't matter

4. Feel free to attend church and on the way home, give
   somebody the middle finger for texting and almost
   crashing into you

The bottom line is everyone communicates differently because everyone has different experiences in life and everyone should be able to express themselves how they want because everyone has a view and everyone and their views matter.

Little Dick Problems

Since we talked about Big Dick Problems, I guess it's only fitting that my mind circled back to dicks again, but this time it has to do with Little Dick Problems. This is a little awkward for me because when I started this book, I wasn't sure where I was gonna take it and I definitely wasn't planning on writing another book about the all-so-important topic of sex…especially not about big dicks and little dicks.

To be fair to the people I'm about to mention in this section, this is only my view based on what I know about dicks and yachts. Yes, I said dicks and yachts.

I have seen a crazy thing in the world of wealthy men. I have seen a man buy a magnificent yacht only to turn around and sell it a couple years later. Why? Why spend hundreds of millions of dollars to purchase and completely renovate an expensive lot only to turn around and sell it?

Because you have a little dick.

I think so because of the yacht-process. Hear me out on this one...

A wealthy man buys a yacht. We will call him Prince John or Prince for short. Prince buys a yacht for $50 million dollars and then pumps another $50 million into it to make sure it is exactly what he wants and what will make everybody's heads turn. It's a beautiful piece of art. It's a 350-foot beautiful, eye-catching piece of art...but it's not good enough anymore.

It's not good enough anymore because another wealthy man, we will call him Jack, has just put his gorgeous, $150 million dollar yacht in the water and guess what? That mutha fucka is 360 feet!

Did you see what just happened? Let me slow walk you through it to see if you get my point on your own without me leading you…

1. Prince spent $100 million dollars for a 350-foot yacht

2. Jack spent $150 million dollars for a 360-foot yacht

3. Prince sells his yacht and has plans to spend $200 million dollars to build a 375-foot yacht.

Alright, Reader. What do you think? Do you see the numbers? Do you see the Dick Envy?

That's okay if you don't and that could be a number of reasons. One reason is you don't care about yachts, another is you just don't see it and another reason is you don't have a dick.

Anybody with a dick, and that's all you men out there, can plainly see somebody has a small penis. Somebody has a small one and is trying to make himself and his penis appear to be larger than life and he is using his money to try and achieve this

goal.

Just so we're clear: I don't have dick envy and I'm not

hating on men who have a lot of money.

I just like to observe shit and speak on it. You can call me

something like a mailman because all I do is deliver the mail…I

don't write it.

What I have observed about yachts is the same thing a

female journalist observed. She said "the world of yachts and

dicks is an obvious one." Why am I talking about dicks again?

I'm talking about it because everything on this planet is

based on sex and us men need to stop doing stupid shit 1) with

our dicks and 2) the way we represent our dicks. I mean, that's a

waste of resources.

The world of little dicks, rich men and yachts has gotten so

ridiculous, I've heard somebody recently literally purchased an old

US Navy Destroyer ship for several million dollars and pumped

another several hundred million dollars into it in an attempt to

guarantee no other rich guy has a bigger dick, I mean a bigger

yacht, than he has! A fucking Navy Warship?!?

I guess I can say my interest in this space is a little

personal, because I am interested in buying yachts but for a

different reason. A reason that has nothing to do with displaying

wealth or inaccurately displaying dick size…

I would like to buy them and travel and let people who

don't have access to yachts travel on them. I want everyone to be

able to put their finger on a dream so they know what it feels like

and so it can become a real thing in their minds.

Before ending this section, I have to add one more

disclaimer: I'm not saying rich white guys with super-yachts all

have small dicks and I don't care.

I just want to make people aware of all the nuances and quirkiness and drama that surrounds dicks. Is it a coincidence that all the super-yacht owners who are known to buy and sell yachts tend to buy and sell them based on whether theirs is the biggest one?

Is it a coincidence as men get older and richer, they ditch the wife who helped them build their wealth and get an attractive, new wife who is typically in her 20's? Speaking of this phenomenon, I don't know what Donald Trump's 1st wife looked like, but I can guess she wasn't an ex-super model who was 25 years younger than he was!

Is it a coincidence there was a wealthy man who wanted to build a big skyscraper who had to 1st inquire into how big was the tallest one and after he got the answer, he told the architect to design one that was "way bigger than the current biggest one"?

Is it a coincidence men over 70 years old don't realize how ridiculous and obvious they are when they decide to buy a brand-new, expensive sports car…only to cruise around driving 10 mph under the speed limit?

Is it a coincidence men love to buy a pickup truck and then put the biggest tires possible on it, get a lift kit to make it sit up another 2 feet and make the exhaust as excruciatingly loud as possible?

Is it a coincidence men love to buy cars with nice sound systems only to rebuild it and add another 2 million watts to it so that when the volume is only on number 3 their back window, the mirrors and the entire car shakes violently to the deafening sounds of the bass?

Is it a coincidence men love to buy cars and put the shiniest, cleanest, most expensive rims on them they can find?

Alright, I've rambled long enough with examples, thoughts and other random shit that was on my mind. I hope you enjoyed it and yes, I think "67" is the final "single" book in this series.

I said "single" because I also have a Personal Development Plan, a Business Development Plan and a Value Retention Plan in the makings.

Doggie-Style

I never realized how much dog's influence our lives until I was sitting here thinking about doggie-style.

We call a certain sexual position doggie-style because it is the missionary-style of dogs and that got me to thinking about our similarities. We are more common to dogs than we think, I think.

Funny story: I knew this guy who had a big, Great Dane type of dog. I don't know remember his name, but for the sake of creativity, let's call him Great. His dog was friendly with other dogs and was the dog version of a human, well, dog.

One day, somebody came over and had a little, white, fluffy female dog. Don't know her name either, so let's just call her Little. Our friend wanted to tie her dog up outside while we were inside playing and we said it would be okay as long as she was tied up far away from Great.

We told her to keep her away from Great because the bitches love him. Now, before you get mad at me for using the "b" word, the term for a female dog is officially "bitch". I could go on about how cusswords aren't as bad as people claim, but I won't. I won't because I have a funny story about a little, white, fluffy bitch named Little and a Great Dane named Great...

The dogs are tied up on 2 different sides of the steps leading into the back door. Great is trying his hardest to get to her and she's trying her hardest to get away from him and inside the safety of the house with us.

We get done playing and go outside and we saw some of the craziest shit I personally have seen in my life: Great and Little were standing there butt-to-butt and Great had a mischievous, guilty look on his face.

Upon further inspection, they were stuck together. You see, Great had humped Little and he couldn't get his Great Dane dick out of her. They were facing but to butt because he, in an attempt to get away, had simply stepped over her and turned around to leave...but obviously couldn't.

We were around 14 or 15 and knew about sex, but not like 14- or 15-year-old kids today know about it. We did know boy dogs have dicks and girl dogs have some sort of vagina, but what we didn't know is a dick, or at least a dog dick, could get stuck inside one.

We thought it was funny, but not funny. We heard you are supposed to pour water on dogs to separate them and we quickly got some water and threw it on them. The only thing that happened was they both got wet.

We then tried to call Great and encourage him to come get a doggie treat in an attempt to have him pull away from her and all that happened was the more he pulled, the more Little's back legs were lifted up off the ground while Great just stood there wishing he had the doggie treat.

While he was standing there thinking about doggie treats, she was standing there, back legs still elevated, looking at us as if to say, "Please stop calling him! Every time you call his dumb-ass, it feels like he's pulling my dog-gina inside out!!!"

Eventually we got them separated. I don't know if Little got pregnant or not and I'm quite sure Great didn't care. He got some sex, a quick cool-down of water and a doggie treat.

That example showed how similar we are to dogs in a number of ways. How about another list?

1. Doggie style: we humans love us some doggie-style sex

2. Once the man busts a nut, he's done. He's ready for a treat, something healthy like a Gatorade and a ham-and-cheese sandwich.

Other than that, I'd be stretching it to try and find more similarities. I could use the bitch reference, but since this is supposed to be a book with "a little more class and holiness" because, well, I guess because I'm a Christian and I'm not supposed to use too much cussing...I'll leave that shit alone.

Speaking of similarities with animals, check out this next topic...

One Chromosome

They say humans have 23 chromosomes in our DNA. This DNA/chromosome is what makes us human. Apparently, each chromosome has different characteristics.

One chromosome determines whether we are a male or female, one determines eye color, one determines hair texture, one determines...you get what I'm saying. I'm talking about chromosomes because scientists are trying to tell us humans and monkeys only have one chromosome that differentiates us.

I think they are full of shit, wasted their scientific degrees and don't deserve to be called legitimate professionals. I think they are full of shit and are from Satan. Let me elaborate...

I'm not saying scientists who think humans could possibly be related to monkeys are satanic. I'm saying that train of thought sounds like something Satan's stupid-ass would try and push on society.

He would love it if our schools and professional scientists used all their brain-power and facts and "proved" humans and monkeys are scientifically related. He would love it because that goes directly against God and the Creation Story.

Before I just dismiss science nerds and Satan, let's look into the validity of their view…

Alright, imagine a monkey standing next to a human. Do you think they are similar? What similarities do you see? I'll bet you see 2 beings who:

1. can stand-up straight,

2. have hands with 5 fingers,

3. have feet with 5 toes,

4. have hair on their bodies and that's all, folks.

Am I to believe after looking at that list, a scientist with a degree in all-things-scientific, came to the rationale decision that humans and monkeys are related? That has got to be some of the dumbest shit a smart person could say!

In general, all 4-legged animals who don't have hooves have 5 "fingers". They may be finger-like or look like claws, but either way, there's five of whatever the fuck you want to call it and they can all stand upright, but that doesn't mean we're related.

I know one chromosome can make a difference, but if science wants me to believe if we could take a monkey and replace one chromosome with a human chromosome that he would function like a human, it won't happen. I will never think that and you sound like a human who had one chromosome replaced with a monkey chromosome!

Am I to believe a monkey will be able to search the web or watch a television show and know exactly what's going on? These hairy cousins of yours, not mine, can't even say a simple word like "marijuana" and you want me to somehow believe a monkey will be able to do and say all of those things if you just tamper with one chromosome?

You are out your monkey-ass mind if you think that or think I'm gonna fall for that monkey shit! Why am I wasting my time talking about monkeys?

I'm talking about them, and I love talking about this topic, because schools and science are able to teach that bullshit about evolution in our schools and presenting our kids with so-called scientific facts and people who believe in God and the Creation story aren't able to have the Bible teach them about another more accurate view of how humans and life began.

The Bible is a book series full of actual, scientific data and historically accurate proof of the Creation story. Why wouldn't we want our children to grow up and learn about their origins from a true, scientifically-supported and historically-proven source?

You know my answer, but I'm gonna let each of you come up with your own answer. Just remember: if you fall for the evolution story, instead of having a human son or daughter, according to science you could realistically have a baby who is a cross between a human and its' distant, evolutionary cousin...the monkey!

Summary and Private Matter Bonus Essay

That's all I got for "Book 67". It was an attempt to not have a book series with 66 books like the Bible. Upon finishing it, I realized I didn't actually have 66 books prior to this one because the autobiography has 2 versions so that's technically 1 book.

That realization made me realize I didn't actually have to write this book because I really only had 65 prior to this one and NOW I actually have 66 books!

Oh well, too late now. The reality is the Bible and this Bible-based, book series both have 66 books and that's something I was trying to avoid so I didn't look hypocritical. I can't change it now. I already tried…

Check out the Private Matter Bonus Essay on random shit. If fits with the random theme of this book. Check it out, Reader, and thanks for readin':

RANDOM SHIT

Thought: If the Earth is round, why don't people on the bottom half of the Earth fall off? Aren't they technically upside-down? Is the pull of gravity heavier for them?

Saying: "Snitches get stitches." That means if you tell on somebody and they find out...yo' ass is gonna get fucked up and need some stitches.

Saying: "I want some head." It does not mean you are hungry and want a head of lettuce, a head of cabbage or anything to do with a literal head...unless you are talking about a dick head. That's because this saying means you want to get your dick sucked.

Saying: "If you hang with a lame, you'll walk with a limp." That means if you hang with somebody long enough, you will eventually act just like them. This one is literal...but not literal. The word "lame" in this context means "a person who isn't doing shit, a buster, a clown" but it also works in this saying because someone who is literally lame literally walks with a limp.

Thought: The word "fuck" is probably the most versatile word on the planet, second only to "shit." It means sex, as in, "Let's fuck." It's used to emphasis or to stress any point you ever want to make, as in, "I'm serious! Leave me the fuck alone!" It is a noun because it describes a person, as in, "He's a dumb fuck." It describes a direction or can be used as an instruction, as in, "Get the fuck out of here and go *that* fucking way." It fills in any blank you have in a sentence, as in, "I'm mad as fuck

Saying: "He don't believe fat meat is greasy." That means you have a hard time understanding the truth. This saying is usually used when someone doesn't believe they will get fucked up. For example, if your neighbor keeps letting his dog shit in your front yard, even after you've told him that both him and his dog will get fucked up...the truth is that one day, if it keeps happening, they both will get fucked up. Well, one of these days when you've had enough of the bullshit and you fuck both of them up...your neighbor and his dog will understand that you meant what you said. You were telling the truth.

Saying: "I will bust his head open to the white meat!" That means you are angry enough to hit somebody on they head so hard their skull busts open like a coconut; leaving the brain, aka "the white meat", exposed.

Saying: "That's not what I meant" means, "That's *exactly* what I meant."

Thought: If the 1st English immigrants that came to America hadn't wiped out almost every form of wild, carnivorous animal on the North American continent, America would be a scary ass place to be. There would be bears, wolves and mountain lions in our backyards, front yards and alleys. I know I would *never* set the trash out front on the curb at nighttime by myself.

Saying: "It's just a white lie." That means its's still a lie, but it's so politely sneaky and deceptive that you don't really feel like it's a lie.

74

75

www.ingramcontent.com/pod-product-compliance
Lightning Source LLC
Chambersburg PA
CBHW061305250726
48653CB00002B/780